BORN MAGIC

Why living an aligned life feels so hard and what to do about it.

SARA WALKA

The Sisters Enchanted®

ISBN 979-8-9858148-4-2 (paperback)

ISBN 979-8-9858148-6-6 (hardcover)

To Scarlett and Adam. You were definitely born magic. Never forget it.

"Nobody looks like what they really are on the inside. You don't. I don't. People are much more complicated than that. It's true of everybody."

-Neil Gaiman, The Ocean at
the End of the Lane

Contents

Introduction

A laundry list of stories

This is a book about you. A book about living an aligned life as an adult. But, to get to that, we must travel back in time and explore childhood.

I'll start.

At around fifteen or sixteen I was sitting at the lunch table with a group of friends. I was never a very outgoing kid but always had a few friends to hang with in social situations like this one. On this particular day I had been reading a book and was fully engrossed in it. I don't remember much about what was happening but I know I pulled that book out at lunch ready to dive in and turn another page.

"You're such a freak."

This is what my best friend at the time had to say to me when she noticed I was not paying one bit of attention to the conversation. To this day I have no idea what they were talking about.

I do know this: I put the book away and never read a book for pleasure at school again.

Let's kick it back further to the first time I was called an asshole. Actually, I think it's the only time I've worn that crown. I was ten. A family member asked me to hold a Christmas tree straight and centered in the holder while that family member anchored it in place. I was ten. I couldn't hold it up straight.

It's fleeting moments like this that create the inner story about who you are. Your strengths, your weaknesses, the good and the bad about you.

I have a laundry list of stories just like the ones I shared from as early as age six to as late as twenty-two. And I bet you do too.

As people fumble through life in their formative years, they have internal and external skills that develop. Our society is built around the notion that these skills develop in a linear fashion on a predictable timeline and for most people, that isn't the case. So when we don't fit in or meet some random standard that's been set, it is brought to our attention. That moment in time creates a lasting story.

In these pages you'll hear about this and about how it impacts the life you are living today. I believe that all of us have the ability to live a life that feels alive, relaxed, and fun. This is what an aligned life looks like. When your inner desires and your outer world match they are in alignment.

This book is best read with a cup of tea, a cozy blanket, and a pen and paper. Take breaks, cry, and release your grip on what was. To make space for what will be, you must know in your heart of hearts that you were Born Magic and are here to create a life that feels aligned with who you are. And who you are is absolutely brimming with magic.

There is a structure to this book that will help you to move through what you experience and apply what you've read. Here is an outline of that structure:

5i Expansion:

This is the framework I developed to help people live with more intention, intuition, and everyday magic so they can live a life that feels aligned, abundant, and relaxed even when uncertainty and chaos are running rampant like the gremlins they are. It is a rhythm-based framework created around Sacred Seeing, Modern Mysticism, and Developmental & Cognitive Psychology. The framework is taught in depth with the practices to support people in living it in my popular program, Holistic Witchery. I mean it when I say you were Born Magic — and this framework is the portal to remembering that. At the end of each chapter I'll loop you into which part of the framework the chapter aligns with and give you a short bit of guidance on what to do along the journey.

Here's an overview of the framework for you:

Intention- How do you want to feel? The stories we tell ourselves impact what we think we're capable of, what we can imagine is possible, and the emotions running through our energy. Instead of starting with goals, we always start with intention. And intention is feeling based.

Integration- What actions can you take to feel this way? The stories you're carrying and whether or not you hold them as truth will dictate the actions you take. Sometimes you'll know what you should do but you won't do it and sometimes you won't know where to begin. Your ethereal energy centers hold these stories.

Insight- How is your past impacting your present and how is that creating your future? This is called shadow work. Your past, present, and future selves are all walking together all the time. The journey to living in alignment requires you to reconcile this.

Ideation- How can you create your desired way of being in a way you haven't yet considered? How can you open yourself to possibility? This is where you connect to your magic and cast the spells that will create a new way of seeing the path ahead of you.

Intuition- What does your soul know? What is your gut telling you? The more you deepen into Intention, Integration, Insight, and Ideation, the stronger your intuition will be. You'll learn self-trust and you'll stop second guessing yourself.

Included in the back of the book you'll find 5i Templates to help you put this framework into place right away.

Journal Prompt:

At the end of each chapter there will be a journal prompt. My top tip for journaling is to try and avoid overthinking your response (hello, Captain Obvious). If you struggle with this or struggle to get started, set a timer for three minutes and write about anything at all, even if that means describing the room around you. Then, try again another day. With enough time the thoughts will begin to leave your beautiful mind and land on paper.

On occasion a prompt will ask you to visualize something, like your future. If you are a person who is not able to visualize or struggles to visualize, logically create the thought and use journaling to record those thoughts.

Here are a few prompts to get you started:

What does the phrase, Born Magic, mean to you?

What fears are coming to the surface from what you've read so far?

What are you excited about as you prepare to move forward in this book?

Embodiment:

The stories, emotions, and rememberings that swell up within you while reading this book need a place to go. I will suggest an embodiment activity at the end of each chapter to get you standing up and doing something. Let everything move through you. These stories and the emotions tied to them have taken up enough space and it's time for them to hit the road. Aside from the embodiment activity I list, I find it helpful to do something that makes me break a sweat when I've been digging into my inner stories. Sometimes this is hiking and sometimes it's sitting in a sauna. All that matters is that you sweat it out.

On the other end of the embodiment spectrum is calming the body. Swaying, gently rubbing your hands down your arms (sort of like petting a dog or cat), and wiggling your arms and legs around are soothing strategies. These give your body a sense of safety, comfort, and presence.

Incorporate one or more of these ideas into your daily life as you nurture your soul, write the next part of your story, and come home to yourself.

Here are more ideas to get you started:

Moving Energy Out- dancing, hiking, walking, jumping jacks, stomping, jumping, arm windmills, running, rapidly shaking your body all about

Calming and Regulating Energy- swaying, petting, neck rolls, gently wiggling, deep breathing, rubbing hands together

Make Magic:

This section will include a hands on activity or ritual to help you create an anchor that ties you to the work you are doing. Life is made of small and big rituals and we'll intentionally create these moments as we move through the book.

Here's where I want you to start:

Create a Quest Pack that you carry with you so you're ready to create these moments when you find an unexpected moment amidst the chaos of life.

It will serve as your reminder to make space for yourself, your vision, and your intuitive self to shine.

Instead of snacks that belong in a garbage pail, questionable beauty products, and loose change, we want you carrying around a Quest Pack that will support you in the unexpected quiet moments, the inevitable chaos of life, and everywhere in between. Some ideas:

- Your Quest Bag, tote, basket, backpack
- Journal and pen and/or notepad
- Water bottle, Earbuds, Snacks
- Oracle, Tarot, or Affirmation Cards
- Tokens of significance like crystals, jewelry, etc.
- Something cozy, like a blanket, shawl, sweatshirt
- Book, magazine, article to read
- Craft project, like knitting, that's easy to grab and go
- Coloring book and crayons or colored pencils
- Picnic blanket or beach towel

Real Life Story:

From doctors to retail managers to retired women to stay-at-home moms, I've worked with thousands of women at The Sisters Enchanted and have had the massive privilege to witness their stories and their transformations.

Throughout the book are just a few of those stories.

Many people in our community come to us when they find themselves at a crossroads. These are women who want to confidently pursue their desires, create lives that feel enchanted, and deepen into secular spirituality.

These women value personal growth and development, authenticity, and open-mindedness. Even though many of the women in our community don't feel like they belong in many traditional communities, they find a sense of belonging at The Sisters Enchanted. They are resilient, have adventurous spirits, and value the freedom to live a life untethered from the nonsense societal norms and expectations that make everything feel so damn hard.

I know you'll see yourself in their stories. Welcome home.

Are you ready? Let's go.

Chapter One

Here's where things go sideways

Why is it that some seven-year-olds are able to keep their rooms clean or organize their folders and backpacks while some aren't?

Why is it that some seventeen-year-olds can manage every bit of the high school experience flawlessly while others can't remember their lunch money, homework, or what class they are supposed to be going to even after three years of doing the same thing each and every day?

Why is it that Kim at the office can find the time to bake homemade cookies for the breakroom, do yoga every morning, and take tiny humans to soccer while you can barely remember what day of the week it is?

The answer lies in executive function skills.

These are the skills that help you organize things and ideas, start and complete tasks, manage multiple ideas at one time, and understand the way other people around you are thinking.

Now this gets interesting: these skills develop in various capacities anywhere between the ages of three and eighteen, and aren't fully developed until age twenty-five for many people.

I'm simplifying and distilling this idea down for the purpose of the book, but this should bring us to a screeching halt.

Some people learn to start tasks all on their own as young as six years old. Others may not develop this skill until they are twelve. Let's do the math: that is a six year timeframe.

Some people will learn to manage a calendar and break big tasks into smaller ones as young as thirteen, and others may be twenty-five before this skill is fully developed. Twelve years. There are twelve years for this skillset to fully form.

Every-freaking-thing.

What does this have to do with living an aligned life?

The first step to living an aligned life is deciding what "aligned life" means for you.

What does it look like? What does it FEEL like? What do YOU want to feel like?

Sounds easy enough, right?

Here's where things go sideways (and where we circle back to executive function skills)... we can't answer any of these questions in a truly authentic way because we are buried under the stories of what we learned to be true about ourselves in childhood.

Our frame of reference and how big we can dream is inhibited by what we learned, from a young age, that we are or are not good at. And who we should and shouldn't be based on the feedback we received about ourselves along the way.

The development of your executive function skills, and whether or not they met the expectations of the grown ups around you at any point, created your inner dialogue and what you think to be true about yourself. These skills impact every action you take and decision you make, impacting every area of your life.

For eighteen years or more of your life you learned what you are and are not capable of through the lens of external expectation.

Read it again: for eighteen years or more of your life, your formative years, you learned what you are and are not capable of through the lens of external expectation.

Sit with that for a minute.

The cherry on top of this rubbish sundae is that these standards were all created to create standard humans. If you're reading this, you're anything but standard.

And that's a very good thing.

* * *

Imagine that a woman named Christine was a child who was always yelled at for having a messy room as a kid. At school Christine was praised for being the one who took charge and helped her peers. In fact, she often finished her work early and went on to help other people. Group projects as a teenager? In the bag. Christine made sure the whole team got an A even if it meant she did all the work.

It's possible that Christine's executive function skills as related to organizing STUFF developed later in life. Or, maybe that area of executive functioning isn't a strong one for her.

What Christine learned is that she is bad at taking care of her stuff but receives high praise for taking care of others.

As an adult, Christine believes an aligned life is one in which support is reciprocal. It feels like being fully supported by her friends, co-workers, and family members. An aligned life is one in which she doesn't have to fight for time to herself or to explore her passions or do something wild like go on vacation with her girlfriends for a week. She feels unburdened and free to say yes to herself.

Christine intends to feel fully supported in all areas of life. This is the intention she has set.

Alas, Christine is not taking care of herself; but her family, co-workers, and friends are very pleased with how much she shows up for and takes care of them.

Do you see where I'm going with this?

* * *

From the early years of life we absorb an external standard for how things should be and who we should be that becomes our inner dialogue. Even if we intend to feel a new or different way, that inner voice keeps playing and will sabotage you every step of the way.

The stories you create about yourself throughout your formative years, particularly around what you are and are not good at, lead you to strive for a perfection standard set by somebody else. One that has nothing to do with who you are or the values you never stopped to develop. And one that actually may have played out entirely differently had you been allowed to write your own strengths and weaknesses story along the way.

"Your soul's purpose and what an aligned life actually looks like for you are buried beneath your whole life to date.

But here's the magic: your capacity for growth, self-discovery, and transformation is infinite. You are not bound by the limitations and expectations imposed on you in childhood.

It's time to rewrite your inner dialogue. It's time to challenge the stories that have held you back and redefine what you are truly capable of. It's time to dig deep, uncover your values, and align your life with what brings you joy, fulfillment, and a deep sense of purpose.

Yes, it will take effort. Yes, it will feel uncomfortable. But the rewards are immeasurable. When you break free from the constraints of external expectations and embrace the truth of who you are, you open up a world of infinite possibilities.

Your aligned life is not a distant daydream. It's a tangible reality waiting to be created. It starts with acknowledging the influence of your younger years and consciously choosing to break free from those stories. There is nothing wrong with you and there never was.

With each step you take towards living in alignment with your true self, your executive function skills evolve because when you focus on what lights you up and your strengths, everything gets easier, your inner dialogue transforms, and your capacity for joy, abundance, and authentic connection expands.

You have the power to rewrite the narrative of your life. Embrace it. Embrace the journey of self-discovery and liberation. Your aligned life is calling, and it's time to answer with a resounding YES.

5i Expansion:

The first i is Intention.

"A thing intended; an aim or a plan" or "the healing process of a wound". I love the second half of that definition. To discover ourselves and the energy we want to embody and live in this lifetime is the ultimate healing adventure.

A common pitfall in intention setting is choosing one based on an external expectation rather than what you truly value, believe, and desire.

For example, if Christine from our story never really thinks about her body too much, happily puts on a bathing suit, and generally feels healthy, goes on to set an intention to feel healthier and attaches a goal to lose twenty pounds, she's unlikely to put much effort into bringing this to reality. Why? Because she doesn't particularly believe she needs to change.

It's a good bet that someone around her (cough, cough, ALL OF SOCIETY — oops, I turned my shouty caps on) made her think that to be valued, she needs to look or act a certain way. Plus, so many of us have been taught that we simply aren't good enough to trust ourselves and need to seek answers from someone else who knows better.

This is why so many people fail to achieve their goals and realize their intentions — because they are based on some external noise and not an internal compass. To set an intention for yourself on the road to creating a life that feels fully aligned to who you are, ask yourself if how you want to feel is based on YOU or on some external standard.

I teach intention setting in conjunction with working with the rhythms of a lunar cycle. The moon has a predictable rhythm that creates space for us to experience the full depth of feeling and emotion that comes with discovering how we want to feel. Ever know for sure what you want and desire and then suddenly feel lost and confused again? Yeah, me too. The rhythm of the moon supports us in this full range of knowing, assuredness, and emotion.

This whole coming home to yourself is a journey. Luckily, enchanted journeys and expeditions to soul are my specialty.

Journal Prompts:

How do you want to feel in life? What stories about who you are or how you are, are keeping you from feeling that way?

What do you believe about your ability to set and achieve goals? Why?

What did you want to be when you grew up and, if you gave up on this, what made you do something else?

What do you think the person who 'has it all together' looks like? What do they act like? How do you know they have it all together?

What evidence do you have of being capable of great, big, exciting action?

Embodiment:

Clear a space.

Have you ever seen a pile of rock after a piece of earth has been blasted to make space for a building? If you haven't, it's like a mountain formed where there was previously flat land. Imagine if a contractor tried to build a new shopping plaza on top of that jagged mound? It wouldn't work. The rocks must be removed. And, so must your stories.

Look around your living space and identify the spot that feels most unaligned with who you are. This could be a messy kitchen drawer or it could be an entire room. Maybe it's the photos on the wall where you'd rather hang art or maybe it's the clothes in your closet that leave you feeling frumpy and uncomfortable. Clear the whole thing out and put it back together again in a way that makes you feel at ease just looking at it.

Cleanse it, practice gratitude for the items you are ready to part with, and feel the connection you have to what was shift and release.

Allow this space clearing and restructuring to be the physical model for what you are doing internally. Coming home to yourself is easier when you're doing tangible work that mirrors the intangible. This is the embodiment work; using the physical to represent the internal and shift your energetic and emotional experience.

If you can't do this now, stop and grab your calendar. Schedule it in so you don't distract yourself and skip this step.

Make Magic:

You Need:

- 10 chime candles
- Wooden plaque

Three is a magic number and three three's creates the powerful number nine. It's said that the ancient Greeks saw the number three as a number of harmony, wisdom, and understanding. This invitation will connect you to the power of that number and the power within yourself.

After gathering the supplies, choose nine words to describe your future self.

Using a pin, carve one word into each of the nine candles. Hold each in your hands and visualize yourself in the future embodying those words. Logically create the thought or write it out if you cannot or do not like to visualize.

When you're ready, use a bit of melted wax from the tenth candle (light the candle and drip it) and affix the candles to a wooden plaque or slice of log. Get creative!

Once they are all affixed to the plaque, light the nine candles saying each word as you light each candle. Sit in the energy for a few moments and snuff the candles out, releasing the future vision to the universe.

Place the plaque where you will see it often. Connect with the energy and say the nine words at least once per day. Each time you bring one of the words to life and realize that you have created that feeling or word into being, light that candle and let it burn all the way down.

Do this until all nine words have been realized and all nine candles have been burned to completion. Then, begin again or re-use the plaque for something fresh.

Real Life Story

Nicole B:

"I was about to burn everything down and quit my entire life. I can't do any of this anymore. I want it done!"

This is where I was before I started my journey with The Sisters Enchanted. Totally done.

When I was younger, I was very much into the witchy stuff. I had all the books and dressed the part as a 90s teen. But as I got older I felt like I had to put that part of my life away. It was time to be a grown up, get a job, and do all the things.

Fast forward to 2020 and the pandemic happened.

I had been feeling a bit lost and with all the new-found time I had I was looking around online and saw a deck of tarot cards. It occurred to me that I never actually learned how to read tarot (despite my 90s teen witch moment). Looking online for tips on how to read the cards, I stumbled across Tarot Throwdown (a program taught at TSE), and something about the video and the way it was taught made me think that I could do that. I could learn to read tarot from these people in that way.

Well, this turned out to be a defining moment because after signing up for the tarot class, I joined in on their Expedition to Soul event.

On Day 2 of the event we were invited to make a declaration and choose that moment as one in which we claimed our future. This is what I wanted! I had been looking for a reason to bring that way of life back. My inner teen witch that felt powerful, confident, and in control was ready to re-emerge. This was the rabbit hole and I was ready to dive in.

Nearly two years later I experienced a truly pivotal moment.

I am part of the mastermind that TSE hosts and was talking about all the things I can't do during one of the group meetings.

Sara looked at me through the zoom screen and asked me for the proof that I can't do all these things I had been listing. Where was the evidence that I can't, or couldn't, do what I was talking about?

All I could see was what I wasn't doing, not what I was.

The TSE team helped me to not only see, but celebrate, all the things I have accomplished.

I always had this thought in the back of my mind that I shouldn't try all these things that I actually wanted to do because I was going to fail. If I already knew that I wasn't going to do it right then I shouldn't even bother trying. I had it in my head that all these things I wanted to do (like learn tarot and astrology) were silly.

As an adult I should be focused on advancing my career and getting my house in order, not learning tarot and astrology. That moment where I was forced to look at my life in a different way was the moment I realized that I have basically everything that I have ever wanted.

And, I came to a neutral position on the dream I had been holding of owning my own business. I'm not sure that I really want to do this when I think about it. I enjoy coming home from work and having my home space as my home space.

But now I see that I could totally do a word of mouth thing and maybe get that happening. Releasing the grip on what I 'should be doing' has allowed me to actually begin opening that door of possibility. I pulled up a birth chart for someone at work recently and she was like, "That makes so much sense!"

The celebrations started running through my head: I did that! Maybe I CAN do this! I helped someone have an a-ha!

The list of changes and things I have accomplished since becoming part of the TSE world goes on!

- I was able to have a difficult conversation with my former stepfather who I have a strained relationship with
- I bought a house
- I surprised myself with my ability to do things to the house including renovating my kitchen and doing a lot of it on my own
- I just finished my basement remodel and even tore a tree stump out of my yard all by myself so I could put a firepit in (this happened when I first joined the mastermind at TSE and it was like the universe testing my resolve to move forward, and move right on through that test!)
- I have also been able to look at my life differently and stop being so overwhelmed by stress and issues at work, it just doesn't bother me like it used to now that I fully realize that I am not my job

Speaking of my job, a few people at work have definitely noticed a change in me. You could tell that I was unhappy, that I was angry, and kind of done with it all before my time with TSE.

Now people tell me that I seem lighter, that I'm "here but not SO HERE" that anything is actually bothering me anymore. I seem happy now. That is fun feedback to receive because I was not a happy person at work, like at all.

I am grateful that I found all of your programs when I did because I was not in a good place but didn't know how to get myself out and knew that it could be better.

I'm glad I took a chance on myself each time a new opportunity was presented and thankful that you made everything so comfortable and easy. There was no pressure to do it right or on time which allowed me to keep taking chances on myself and growing.

Being able to receive specific feedback from the mastermind and have someone bounce back what I was saying but with truth attached to it was incredibly helpful and I appreciate the opportunity.

Your soul's purpose and what an aligned life actually looks like for you are buried beneath your whole life to date.

Chapter Two

Cue dramatic music

People take action based on what is safe. Humans, you and me, we like to feel safe.

In the previous chapter, Christine set her intention to feel fully supported.

This feeling, though, is entirely outside of her comfort zone and what feels like safety to her.

She already knows that she controls the result if she takes charge and takes care of everyone. She knows what will happen, how everyone will react, and exactly what to expect. She knows this because she's been doing it her whole life and has evidence to back this up.

Christine might be burnt out, frustrated, and crying in the bathroom but at least she is in control. This feeling of control equates to safety.

If Christine decides to lean into her intention of feeling fully supported this will rock every boat in her life and the consequences of that are unknown. She'll have to say no, set boundaries, and trust others. Wild, I know.

Taking action to live an aligned life that feels connected to a deeper soul's desire is hard. There's no way around it. When a person feels out of alignment or like they aren't living a life that feels like magic, it is because they are living a life based on what they know. Living a life based on what you don't know, that is in alignment with a way you don't yet know how to experience, is like stepping into an alternate reality that you can't begin to know the ins and outs of.

Old way of being = safe.

New way of being = not safe.

This picture will stop you from taking action on your new intention again and again and again.

What you learned about yourself from a young age through early adulthood created the picture you have of yourself.

Taking action on your new intended way of being requires integrating that intention into who you are now.

If who you are now doesn't have space or capacity for that new intended way of being, you can't integrate it and you won't take action on it. Well, not effective and long lasting action.

Think about a puzzle that is already put together. You are that puzzle. In order to change the image made up of lots of tiny bits, you have to first remove the ones that need changing. That feels hard and uncomfortable because you've already worked so hard to put this exact puzzle together. If you're happy with it, leave it. If not, roll up your sleeves because you have some work to do.

A barrier people often run into right around now is the fear that changing requires burning everything down. The fear that an old life can't exist with a new life.

The only two things that can't exist together are the old ways of being and seeing yourself and the new ways of being and seeing yourself. The life you want to live and the energy you want to embody can live in your existing life because that life will start to adapt to your new energy, your new essence, your new found sense of enchantment. If you act with confidence and believe in yourself, of course.

Energy is adaptable. People are adaptable. Circumstances are adaptable.

* * *

Christine tells her co-workers that she will no longer be working late to finish the project. She tells her family that she will no longer be cleaning up after them.

It's Friday at 3pm and the work project isn't done.

It's Sunday afternoon and no one has put away the laundry or done the dishes.

Cue dramatic music.

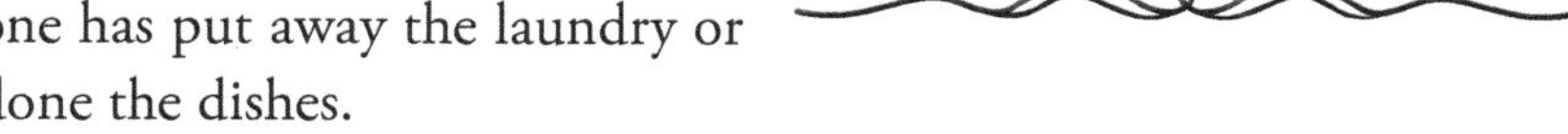

Christine has two choices. Hold her boundary and new-found intention, or cave and pick up the slack. Feel fully supported or support everyone else?

If Christine has not done the inner work necessary to create a rhythm of expansion and a life of alignment, she's going to cave.

Why? Because she doesn't know what will happen if she doesn't. It feels unsafe. And, if you remember from Chapter One, Christine learned from an early age that she is very good at helping others. All the praise she gets for being superwoman doesn't hurt either, even though she's dying for a life that feels like hers.

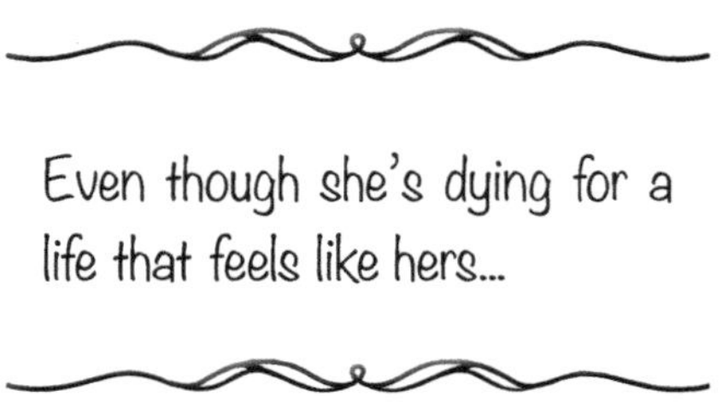
Even though she's dying for a life that feels like hers...

A life that feels joyful, abundant, and relaxed. A life that she believes only exists in a daydream.

However, deep down, Christine knows that daydreaming is not enough. It's time to bridge the gap between her yearnings and her reality. It's time to shatter the illusion that a life of fulfillment and authenticity is beyond her reach.

As Christine contemplates her choices, her mind races with questions. Will she be seen as selfish or irresponsible? Will she disappoint those who have come to rely on her unwavering support? The weight of these expectations threatens to anchor her in the familiar, in the safety of her old way of being.

But something stirs within Christine—a flicker of courage, a whisper of her true desires. She realizes that she can no longer deny herself the possibility of a life that feels like hers. She understands that stepping into the unknown is the only path to unlocking her true potential.

Christine takes a deep breath and makes a decision. She chooses herself. She chooses to honor her intention of feeling fully supported, even if it means unraveling the comfortable tapestry she has woven.

In the face of uncertainty, Christine must summon the strength to navigate the choppy waters of transformation. Doubts and fears swirl around her, threatening to drown out her newfound resolve. Yet, with every step forward, she discovers reserves of resilience she didn't know she possessed.

She embarks on a journey of self-discovery, shedding the layers of her old identity that no longer serve her. It's a process that demands vulnerability, compassion, and a willingness to let go. Christine learns to release the need for control and perfection, embracing the messy and unpredictable nature of growth.

As she redefines her boundaries and communicates her needs, Christine encounters resistance from those accustomed to the old version of her. Some question her motives, while others struggle to adjust to the shift in dynamics. It's an uncomfortable and at times lonely path, but Christine finds solace in the unwavering belief that she is worthy of a life aligned with her deepest desires.

The days turn into weeks, and the weeks into months. Christine's choices and actions begin to reshape her reality. By prioritizing her well-being and setting boundaries, she invites new possibilities and experiences into her life. Relationships transform, as some fall away to make space for those who genuinely support her growth. She discovers hidden talents and passions, rekindling a sense of wonder and curiosity she thought she had lost.

All of this because she chose to take aligned action and create her intentions into being.

And as Christine reflects upon her life, she realizes that the pursuit of a life that feels like hers was never a daydream but a courageous act of self-love. One piece at a time Christine adjusts the puzzle of her life and her inner landscape. Slowly but surely the picture transforms.

Sometimes she is tempted to put back the old pieces or doesn't know what to do next.

That's where the next part of the story comes in.

Journal Prompts:

Where does the feeling of discomfort sit in your body when you start to think about taking action on how you want to feel?

What do you do simply because it feels safe and predictable?

Where do you stop yourself from holding a boundary because you've learned to be the savior and step in and control situations?

Where is there an incongruence in your daily life and the energy you want to embody?

What's the worst that could happen if you said no or just let go of control and put yourself and your desires first?

5i Expansion:

The second i in the framework is Integration.

To integrate is to unify pieces into one whole.

Think of your inner self as a puzzle. You are trying to fit new pieces (your desired way of being) into an existing puzzle. Taking action on your intention requires you to see this disconnect. Remember that the first i was Intention. Once you uncover the life you intend to live, the way you intend to feel, and the energy you intend to embody, you must take action and integrate that new way of being into the life you are currently living.

This is where we meet resistance in ourselves, in the people who love us most (because they get scared just like you), and in the society we live in that isn't built for living a life of joy, abundance, and relaxation. A life of soul alignment.

If our hero Christine sets the intention to feel more relaxed but has a calendar that is jam-packed and is the person everyone calls for help, she will simply not feel relaxed, no matter how much she desires it. To feel relaxed she must begin creating a new puzzle by establishing boundaries, clearing her calendar, and developing a habit of keeping white space. Christine must take action to integrate her intention or goal into herself and her life.

I live in an area of the United States where we don't have a city sewer system. There is a septic tank in my front yard where all the wastewater from my home goes to do its thing. It's underground right between two beautiful maple trees. A few times per year we have to yank baby roots out of the tank because they start to clog everything up. The stories in your energy are like those roots. They run deep and you've gotta' keep checking in and pulling them out.

Identify where your current actions are out of alignment with how you desire to feel and live and then pull out the stories leading to those actions.

Embodiment:

Dance and laugh.

Make it a practice to move your body as often as possible. There are books on the topic and research galore supporting the notion that emotions are stuck in our bodies. Experiences, memories, and stories all live in there taking up valuable space.

Here's a quote from a study on embodiment, "We conclude that emotional feelings are associated with discrete, yet partially overlapping maps of bodily sensations, which could be at the core of the emotional experience. These results thus support models assuming that somatosensation and embodiment play critical roles in emotional processing."[1]

Dance and laughter are the medicine of the masses and can shift your energy in no time. There's a whole form of healing that is done using laughter. Sit and make yourself laugh until you're really laughing. Then you laugh and laugh until you're crying. Finally, you cry until you don't have anything left to cry. It's not easy to laugh on command but you can play some music and bob your head or get up and dance with freedom at any time if the laughter exercise feels like too much.

This is hard work you are doing and brings up A LOT. Dance it out and let all that a-lot-ness flow out through your fingertips and toes and the top of your head. Shake it, twirl it, and drop it like it's hot until your breath is quick and you feel a lightness in your body that signals you're done... for now.

---

1 Nummenmaa, L., Glerean, E., Hari, R., & Hietanen, J. K. (2014). Bodily maps of emotions. Proceedings of the National Academy of Sciences of the United States of America, 111(2), 646–651. https://doi.org/10.1073/pnas.1321664111

Make Magic:

You Need:

- Colored pencils or crayons
- Blank paper

Light a candle and create a calm environment that feels connected and secure.

Think about a truly audacious future goal. Something that feels way too big and wild. Write it on the top of a piece of blank paper.

Put your hands on your lower belly and imagine yourself living this dream. How does it feel? Does it feel safe to live this dream? Write about the feeling or draw it on the paper. Write, "I am capable, I am worthy, I am magic," on the bottom of the paper.

Do this again with your hands on your heart and a new piece of paper and do it a third time with your hands on your head a fresh sheet of paper. Each time writing the goal on the top first.

When you are done you will have three pieces of paper. Notice the stories that come up for you. If they are stories that feel powerful and like the sort of story that will cast a great vision, keep the paper. If you have a story that feels like it needs to be released. Burn that piece of paper (or pieces if there is more than one) and release the story.

If you have a paper or papers remaining, put them in a safe place and revisit them at a later date. Release as you're ready to release. If none of the papers are left, thank the universe or the higher power you believe in and enter back into daily life.

Real Life Story:

Morgan R.

"Where is this coming from, why am I so terrified? This is a question I used to have to ask myself all the time."

People join online programs because they want to see a clear result.

But that's the thing about TSE, it's the foundation for everything. For every clear result that you could possibly want.

Before participating in classes at TSE I had no confidence, had anxiety, went to sleep anxious and fearful and would wake up at 2am with so much stress and anxiety. I would just wake up for things that I didn't need to be waking up for and lay there not knowing the way forward.

Holistic Witchery and Tarot Coach were the first two programs I registered for at TSE. It took me a long time to take the step... should I, shouldn't I? I kept going back and forth.

Fast forward to the present and I'm sleeping all night. I'm sleeping really well, and I can't remember the last time I felt this great. Did TSE teach me how to sleep through the night? No! But what I learned here laid the foundation for easing my mind and body.

I have always procrastinated and had fears of confrontation. Through the shadow work done in the Holistic Witchery program I found out why. It was so simple and in front of my face and if I hadn't done that class I never would have known and wouldn't have stood up for myself.

Where I used to panic, I now apply the 5i's from Holistic Witchery and it all seems so easy.

I have the confidence to say, "oh that's easy, I can do that." The foundation is there because of what I've learned.

I'm a good reminder that you can live the life you've always dreamed of and still have lots of work to do to feel good in that life. I've traveled all of the United States, am self-employed, have money, and take vacations. But when it came to regular day-to-day life and decisions I was so fearful and it was all anxiety inducing.

I have learned to be at peace with myself and in my body in any situation through The Sisters Enchanted programs.

I also learned that I'm really great at manifesting things into my life but wasn't stopping to be grateful for them.

A key game changer for me in my time with TSE has been learning about time.

Life is so LONG and every day can be amazing. You can always start again. There's SO MUCH TIME.

Since learning about time and being intentional with TSE I have so much more time. The time management lessons opened up everything for me.

I used to be so fearful of life ending and now I ask myself about what I can be doing from now to then. I'm excited for the future and wasn't before.

The Sisters Enchanted programming is the FOUNDATION FOR EVERYTHING — for every part of your life.

The last thing I'll note is that a sense of knowing is coming quicker for me that it ever was before. When I'm hearing other people talking or looking at my own situation I can see the way forward or the underlying shadows right away. I used to wait or not know what to do. I was always waiting until the last minute but now I just know and I just take action.

Taking action on your new intended way of being requires integrating that intention into who you are now.

Chapter Three

Deep in a well of emotion

We develop our sense of self based on the caregivers in our lives as children.

If you are a person who has an impact on the lives of young people right now, hold onto your hat because it's about to get bumpy.

Your ability to live an aligned life is impacted by the awareness you have of your emotional wounds and your ability to see them as they are, with neutrality.

Here's the thing though: we aren't taught neutrality.

The statements that run through your subconscious mind about yourself are impacted by how good your caregivers were at staying grounded, present, and neutral.

Do you need to get a cup of tea or a comfy snuggle blanket to process this thought? Go ahead, I'll wait.

Back? Let's keep going. Everything we've covered so far in this book contributes to lack of neutrality. We are swaddled in expectation at birth, carry it in backpacks as kids, and see it plastered on billboards as adults. And the people who impacted you and me as kids had the same experience.

We're all just a bunch of people walking around trying to be a certain way for fear of not being that way. Most people are not naturally good at remaining neutral and refraining from blaming, shaming, and defining their emotions based on what other people around them are doing.

Detaching one's emotional being from the actions of people around you is a learned skill. Releasing expectation of others is also a learned skill.

They may have had the best of intentions and the poorest of outcomes.

The adults you and I were surrounded with as kids taught us everything we know about what makes us good, valuable, and worthy.

Chances are, they, just like you, were doing their best given the stories they had internalized about themselves.

* * *

Christine is a kid who is supposed to be cleaning her room. Instead, she is fiddling around with her toys or trying to soothe her overwhelm by doing something infuriating like peeling the paper off a crayon and making a bigger mess.

"You're making me mad!"

"This isn't that hard!"

"If only you'd focus you'd be done by now!"

What Christine translates this to is the story that she makes people mad because she isn't good at taking care of her stuff and cleaning her room which... allegedly... isn't that hard.

The caregiver in this scenario is not grounded, is not neutral, and is definitely not present. That caregiver is deep in a well of emotion.

A well of emotion that Christine has fallen down and can't get out of.

A caregiver who is easily dysregulated teaches you that you have to be a certain way in order to keep them calm.

Christine, as an adult, will not live her intended way of being and step into a fully aligned life until she has seen this wound from a neutral perspective and accepted it as part of her story. Otherwise, these stories will continue weaving her destiny.

* * *

If you are currently in a position to impact young people, this is where generational change happens. You are not only creating a life of enchantment, abundance, joy, relaxation, and ALIGNMENT for you... no, you are opening this door for all the young people who see you doing it for yourself right now.

Growing into you who you desire to be and creating a life you love isn't selfish, it's the greatest gift you can give the world.

Seeing the open wounds you are carrying and beginning to close the door on what was will allow you to pull yourself out of the tapestry of your life to date and see who you actually are. This insight separates who you were from who you will be.

These stories creep up when you least expect them. Maybe it's a supervisor or a neighbor who is losing their temper or a family member that has reached their limit. The part of a person that is still carrying the stories of childhood and how they contribute to someone else's emotional state will bubble to the surface.

Thoughts like:

> "I should've known."
>
> "Everybody else can do it so why can't I?"
>
> "It's not that hard. I just need to be better."

Shadow work is the process of healing these wounds and is what will clear the way for new stories to take up space in your energy.

By engaging in shadow work, you confront the wounds, beliefs, and patterns that have been unconsciously guiding your life. It's a deep exploration of your subconscious mind, where you uncover the hidden layers of conditioning and trauma that have shaped your self-perception and behavior.

It's not an easy journey. It requires courage, self-compassion, and a willingness to confront uncomfortable truths. But through shadow work, you can release the grip of past wounds and rewrite the narratives that have held you back.

As you heal and integrate these wounded aspects of yourself, you gain the power to see yourself with neutrality. You can embrace your strengths and vulnerabilities, free from the judgments and expectations of others. You become the author of your own story, no longer confined by the limitations imposed upon you.

Shadow work is an ongoing process, a lifelong commitment to self-discovery and growth.

But with each layer you peel away, you create more space for alignment, joy, and authenticity in your life.

Embark on this transformative journey. Open yourself to the shadows, confront the wounds, and embrace the power that comes from healing and reclaiming your true essence. By doing so, you not only transform your own life but also create a ripple effect of liberation and healing for future generations.

The time for neutrality, self-compassion, and generational change is now. Embrace the bumpy road ahead, for it leads to a life of alignment, joy, and boundless possibilities.

Journal Prompts:

What is one thing you believe to be true about yourself that is based on a story and not truth?

What expectations do you think other people have for you and how have they impacted your life and decisions you've made for it?

What expectations do you hold for other people and how are those impacting you?

Examine the word neutrality in the context of your life right now. Where do you lack neutrality? How does that impact your mind and body?

Look at fears you have now. Can you trace those back to moments in time where a dysregulated caregiver imparted their fear or belief on you?

5i Expansion:

The third i is Insight.

Here's one definition of the word, insight: The capacity to gain an accurate and deep intuitive understanding of a person or thing.

Have you ever heard of the term 'shadow work'? This is what we do here. Look at the hidden bits of ourselves and our stories and reclaim them into our wholeness.

There's a tendency to disconnect from the moments and events in life that aren't ideal, but all these little experiences and beliefs are part of how you came to be who you are today. Loving on them just like you would the 'good stuff' is vital to creating an aligned life.

First you decide how you want to feel, then you work on inserting that new way of feeling and being into your life, and then you do shadow work. Zoom out and look at where you didn't go all in on your desired future. What stopped you? What beliefs about yourself or your life that come from a past experience are creating your present reality? This is shadow work.

Christine, the character who represents us all, can do shadow work to understand why she doesn't feel the way she wishes to feel. Then, she'll be ready to re-imagine the way forward, which is the next stop on our journey.

Embodiment:

Begin by crafting a comprehensive list of all the trivialities, the irritations, the distractions that have been draining your energy and diverting you from your true path. These could be negative thoughts, toxic relationships, unhealthy habits, or self-doubt. Anything that hinders your growth or dims your inner light. Write them all down. Include anything you've been tolerating that eats away at you like a termite on your soul.

Next, safely set this list ablaze. As the flames consume the paper, visualize them releasing these negative aspects of your life. You are not just burning a piece of paper; you are symbolically burning away the obstacles that stand between you and your aligned life.

As the fire turns your list to ashes, imagine it doing the same to your burdens, your fears, your limitations. Feel the weight lifting, the shadows receding. In their place, see the fire's light, its warmth, its transformative energy. This is the energy of clearing and making space.

Finally, breathe. Inhale deeply, drawing in the energy of the fire, the promise of new beginnings. Exhale fully, releasing any residual negativity, any lingering doubts. Feel the space you've created within yourself, a space now ready to be filled with positivity, with growth, with alignment to your true self.

A path free of the nonsense you've been tolerating has been laid. A path that leads to the fullest representation of you.

Make Magic:

You Need:

Three pieces of string (like embroidery floss) in three colors

1. Preparation: Find a quiet, comfortable space where you won't be disturbed. Lay out your three pieces of string. Assign each color to represent your past self, present self, and future self. The color assignments can be based on intuition, personal preference, or color symbolism.
2. Reflection: Take a moment to hold each string and reflect on what it represents. For the past self, consider the experiences that have shaped you, the lessons you've learned, and how you've grown. For the present self, focus on your current state, your feelings, your strengths, and areas you're working on. For the future self, envision your goals, aspirations, and the person you aim to become.
3. Braiding: Begin to braid the strings together. As you intertwine the strings, imagine the integration of your past, present, and future selves. Consider how your past experiences have shaped your present and how your present actions are shaping your future.
4. Meditation: As you continue to braid, allow yourself to enter a meditative state. Reflect on the interconnectedness of your past, present, and future selves. Acknowledge that each part is essential in your personal journey and growth.
5. Completion: This braided string is a symbol of your life's journey, a tangible reminder of your continuous growth and evolution. You may choose to keep this braided string in a special place or wear it as a bracelet or bookmark. Whenever you see it, let it serve as a reminder of your past experiences, your present state, and your future aspirations.

Real Life Story:

Karla D.

I once punished my kids for doing crystal meditations, and now here I am growing personally and spiritually with The Sisters Enchanted!

When I was growing up my mother was Wiccan and my father was Catholic. In 1993 my mother died of cancer. When she was sick her coven would bring herbal remedies and my dad's priest would come and pray but nothing worked. When she passed I built walls around myself spiritually.

As an adult I was searching for something, went to therapy for many years, and finally overcame fears. In 2016 I stumbled upon TSE on Facebook and something about Sara and Anna — you guys were just amazing! At this time I was in an abusive relationship and couldn't participate in classes but enjoyed following along on social media. I participated in every free thing that was offered by TSE and it changed my whole life.

One day I was listening to a TSE podcast and the topic was something like having the choice to stay in your current situation or get out. Well, I got out.

I got out of that relationship, moved to Minnesota, and met my soulmate.

That's when I was able to participate in the classes that The Sisters Enchanted hosted and really dive in.

In Holistic Witchery I had an aha moment around setting intentions. Normally I would set my north star goals but I could never achieve them and I didn't know why and couldn't understand.

In Holistic Witchery I put it all together in the 5i Spiral and realized that it's actually SO EASY.

That's been the biggest thing for me.

I'm finally understanding my religion instead of my mom's religion and my spirituality instead of my mom's spirituality. As a kid what I saw in her religion from a child's eyes was scary for me.

The Sisters Enchanted came along and it has been a dream and I thank you so much.

I am trusting people now and I never trusted people before. I would never trust a therapist and now I am. TSE opened that trust. And, I trust myself!

I am blunt (especially at work) and I've learned to hold my tongue so I won't hurt people and while I used to get upset with my kids for doing crystal meditations, I now use crystals to support myself in better communication.

As a person who learns best through listening or watching, the videos and audio that TSE offers have helped me in so many ways.

Your ability to live an aligned life is impacted by the awareness you have of your emotional wounds and your ability to see them as they are, with neutrality.

Chapter Four

Dreaming big isn't easy

Christine sits down to write in her journal, maybe she pulls some tarot or oracle cards, she lights a candle.

What is your future vision? What does your dream future look like? These are the questions Christine is creating space to answer.

She dreams of a future where she is fully supported. One in which she holds her boundaries and when everything goes to hell she calmly goes about her business and allows everyone else to pick up their share of the pieces. She envisions a harmonious home where her family members take responsibility for their own actions and contribute to the household. She imagines open and honest conversations, where emotions are expressed and resolved with compassion and understanding. She sees her co-workers stepping up and taking ownership of their workload and expectations, working collaboratively and supporting one another.

But as Christine delves deeper into her future vision, she realizes that there are aspects she hasn't yet considered. The practical challenges and growth areas that require her attention and effort. She acknowledges that creating a future of full support goes beyond wishful thinking. It requires her to think of solutions she has never considered before.

What Christine doesn't initially dream about is how to create more money so she can hire an assistant. That's because no one she knows has this. But, she allows herself to dream and consider it. She recognizes that financial abundance is a vital aspect of her future vision. She begins to explore strategies and opportunities to expand her income and create the resources necessary to support her desired lifestyle.

She also contemplates the art of effective communication and leadership within her family dynamic. Christine understands that leading a family meeting that doesn't end in tears and eye rolls requires conscious effort and skill. She explores resources on conflict resolution, active listening, and assertiveness to develop her ability to navigate familial discussions with grace and clarity.

In her journey towards an aligned life, Christine realizes the importance of self-expression and speaking her truth. She seeks out courses and workshops that help her develop her voice and communicate assertively and confidently in her workplace. She understands that by honing her communication skills, she can establish healthy boundaries, articulate her needs, and contribute more effectively to the team.

But Christine's future vision is not limited to external factors and practical strategies. She recognizes the importance of inner work and embodiment practices. She yearns to release the heavy burden of guilt that weighs her down and hinders her progress. Through meditation, mindfulness, and self-reflection, she commits to developing embodiment practices that cultivate self-compassion and allow her to let go of guilt. She explores various modalities such as yoga, breathwork, and energy healing to connect with her body and spirit, nurturing a sense of inner peace and alignment. Christine cultivates a relationship with the moon and deepens into ritual as a way to create trust and openness.

As Christine continues to explore her future vision, she realizes that it is a holistic journey of growth and transformation. It requires a balance of practical action and inner work. It demands a commitment to personal development and a willingness to step outside of her comfort zone.

And so, armed with her journal, tarot cards, and a candle, Christine embraces the path ahead. She knows that her dream future is within reach, but it requires her dedication, resilience, and a willingness to continuously learn and evolve.

She understands that the future she envisions is not a static destination, but an ever-unfolding process of alignment, growth, and self-discovery. And as she takes each step, she becomes the creator of her own reality, shaping a future that reflects her deepest desires and honors her authentic self.

* * *

Ideation is the formation of ideas and concepts, a process deeply intertwined with our personal experiences, observations, and executive function skills. It's through ideation that we have the capacity to dream big and envision a future beyond our current circumstances. However, we must acknowledge that dreaming big isn't easy—it can be incredibly challenging.

Allowing ourselves to step outside of our comfort zones and embrace discomfort is essential in the process of dreaming beyond what we already know. It requires breaking free from the safety of what's familiar and venturing into uncharted territory. Only by embracing discomfort can we unlock our full potential and explore the realms of possibility.

When we embark on the journey of creating a new future vision, it's crucial to seek inspiration from those who are already living the future we aspire to. Looking beyond the circle of familiar faces, the individuals who have shaped our inner dialogue and our perception of what's possible thus far, allows us to expand our horizons. By observing and learning from those who have already blazed a trail, we gain insights, strategies, and the courage to push boundaries and forge our own path.

To illustrate the concept of ideation, let's imagine being asked to draw a picture of a planet we've never seen before. Naturally, our initial instinct would be to start with a circle—the common representation of a planet. We might then choose to color it with earth tones or neutral colors, or perhaps we'll let our imagination run wild and paint it blue like Neptune or red like Mars.

However, it's highly unlikely that we would draw this planet as a square or embellish it with pink polka dots. Why? Because our frame of reference, derived from what we have witnessed and experienced, shapes our understanding of what a planet should look like. Our imagination is anchored to our past observations and limited by our current knowledge.

When we aspire to a life we've never lived before, a life that our caregivers did not teach us to envision, we lack a frame of reference for that vision. It feels unfamiliar, foreign, and even unreachable. But it is precisely in this space of the unknown that true ideation can flourish.

The process of ideating on what is possible requires us to introspect and comprehend how our past experiences have shaped who we are today. It calls for a deep understanding of the stories we have internalized and the narratives that need shifting. By recognizing the beliefs, limitations, and self-perceptions that no longer serve us, we open ourselves up to the possibility of creating a future that aligns with our desired state of being. And, if the stories you've been taught along the way are ones that leave you lacking in confidence or second guessing yourself, you'll find this particularly challenging.

Living an aligned life means consciously crafting a future that reflects our true desires, passions, and values. It involves breaking free from the confines of our past experiences and societal expectations, and embracing the potential of what could be. It calls for intentional action, mindful decision-making, and a commitment to personal growth and transformation.

In this quest for alignment, we must embark on a journey of self-discovery. It is through introspection, self-reflection, and a willingness to challenge our current beliefs that we can redefine our frame of reference. By releasing the limitations imposed by our past and embracing the power of our imagination, we become capable of ideating on a future that surpasses what we have experienced and witnessed thus far.

Dare to dream beyond the boundaries of your past. Embrace the discomfort and uncertainty that come with envisioning a new future. Seek inspiration from those who have forged their own paths. Understand the stories that have shaped you, and consciously choose to rewrite the narratives that no longer serve your highest good.

Living an aligned life is a continuous journey, filled with twists, turns, and unexpected discoveries. But through the process of ideation, we have the power to transcend our current reality and manifest a future that is vibrant, fulfilling, and deeply aligned with our authentic selves.

Take a moment to sit with your dreams, your desires, and the vision of the future you wish to create. Let your imagination soar, unburdened by the constraints of your past. Embrace the power of ideation and open yourself to the infinite possibilities that await you on your path to alignment.

Journal Prompts:

What does it look like to feel the way you want to feel? What is your frame of reference for this?

Reflect on your journey of self-discovery so far. What have you learned about yourself through introspection and self-reflection? How have these insights helped you challenge your current beliefs and redefine your frame of reference?

Who are the people that inspire you and have forged their own paths? How have their stories influenced your own journey towards living an aligned life?

Write about a situation where you had to step outside of your comfort zone. What was challenging about this experience? How did it help you grow and what did you learn about your potential?

Take a moment to sit with your dreams and desires. What does the future you wish to create look like? How can you use the power of ideation to manifest this future? Write down your vision in as much detail as possible.

5i Expansion:

The fourth i" in our transformative journey is Ideation. This is the stage where dreams take shape and the seeds of reality are sown. It's the playground of the future, a realm where you can freely experiment with possibilities and envision the life you aspire to live. It's a space where you can draw inspiration from the lives of others who are already living the life you desire, and use their examples as a blueprint for your own journey.

Ideation is the process of assembling the scattered pieces of your life in a new, innovative way. It's like being an artist with a blank canvas, where each stroke of the brush brings you closer to the masterpiece that is your life. It's about daring to dream, daring to disrupt the status quo, and daring to design a life that aligns with your deepest desires and highest values.

However, ideation is not for the faint-hearted or the rigid-minded. A person who declares, 'there's no way this will ever change,' is a person who has yet to unlock the power of ideation. They are stuck in the confines of their current reality, unable to envision a new path forward. But the truth is, there is always a new way forward. Finding it requires a flexible mindset, a creative spirit, and an openness to exploration and experimentation.

This is why ideation is positioned fourth in our framework. It's a crucial step, but it's not the first. It builds upon the foundation laid by the preceding steps. Without first gaining self-awareness, challenging existing beliefs, and aligning with your authentic self, ideation can be a daunting task.

The journey to ideation is like climbing a mountain. The first three steps are about preparing for the climb, understanding the terrain, and aligning with your purpose for the journey. Only then are you ready to ascend to the peak of ideation, where you can survey the landscape of your life from a new perspective and chart a course towards your desired future. It's a challenging climb, but the view from the top makes it all worthwhile.

Embodiment:

Do something new with your body and energy. Paint a canvas, make a vision board, hike a new trail, or swim in the ocean. The choice is yours, but the key here is to choose an activity that is outside of your usual routine.

Why is this important? Because when we disrupt our typical behaviors and the usual actions of our body, we create an opportunity for our mind to break free from its habitual patterns. We open up a space for our mind to explore new territories, to think in different ways, and to generate fresh perspectives. It's like taking a detour on a familiar road - you might discover a beautiful landscape that you've never noticed before.

What activity will you choose to disrupt your routine and stimulate your mind? Remember, it doesn't have to be something grand or complicated. It just needs to be different from what you usually do.

As you engage in this new activity, allow your thoughts to flow freely. Don't try to control or judge them. Just observe them as they come and go. You might be surprised by the creative solutions or innovative ideas that pop into your mind. These could be insights into how you can create a life that is more aligned with your true self.

But don't stop there. Take note of these insights and ideas. Write them down. Reflect on them. How can you apply them to your life? How can they guide you towards your vision of an aligned life?

Remember, vision is not just about seeing the future. It's also about exploring the present in new and unexpected ways. It's about disrupting the familiar to discover the extraordinary. It's about stepping out of the ordinary to step into the extraordinary. Disrupt your routine. You never know what amazing insights and ideas you might uncover.

Make Magic:

Materials Needed:

- Cardstock or thick paper
- Art supplies (markers, colored pencils, paints, etc.)
- A journal and pen
- A quiet, comfortable space for reflection

Instructions:

1. Card Creation: Cut your cardstock into cards of your preferred size. Start with a small number and add more over time.
2. Reflection: Take a moment to reflect on your past and future. Consider the significant events, people, and lessons in your life. Think about where you want to be in the future, your goals, and aspirations.
3. Designing the Cards: Begin to design your cards based on your reflections. Each card should represent a specific aspect of your past or a future goal. You could create cards for specific events or people, or for more abstract concepts like love, success, or growth. Use your art supplies to create images that resonate with you. Don't worry about artistic skill; the important thing is that the images hold meaning for you.
4. Card Interpretation: On the back of each card, write a brief description of what it represents and how it can be interpreted. For example, a card representing a past hardship might suggest resilience and strength in the face of adversity when drawn in a reading. Or, design your card back and write the meanings separately.
5. Using Your Cards: Once you've created your deck, you can use it for self-reflection and guidance. Draw a card when

you need insight or inspiration. Reflect on its meaning and how it relates to your current situation.

6. Continued Creation: Your deck is a living tool that can grow and change with you. Feel free to add new cards as you reach new milestones or set new goals.

Jena S.

I am worthy, I am not just my health, not just a mom. These are parts of me but they aren't me. They don't have to hold me back.

Before The Sisters Enchanted (TSE) I was at a point where I had lost myself completely as a mom caring for my neurodivergent children and my own health issues while trying to navigate everything that comes up in life.

I felt like I had lost myself and with my kids both beginning school full time I didn't know what to do.

I knew that I needed to do something for myself, with my time, and to contribute financially to the household. We had been a single income household for ten years and that had never been part of the plan (but life happened).

After my second pregnancy I developed PMDD and in August 2020 I experienced a significant emotional breakdown. I reached out to my therapist looking for a workbook or a tool to guide me back to myself. I was done not knowing who I was anymore. One thing led to another which led me to TSE.

I started following TSE online in the beginning of 2021 but never had time to get into it and commit to any of the classes.

When 2022 hit (and 22 is my lucky number) I claimed it as my year. This was the year I was going all in on myself!

The 21-day self-care challenge was happening and I was ready to commit. While I had been doing shadow work before this, I finally saw it as something that didn't have to be so daunting. This was affirmed to me by one of the TSE teachers who commented on my challenge participation. I was doing it! And I kept on doing it when the next class came around, Expedition to Soul.

When it came time to register for Holistic Witchery with The Sisters Enchanted I knew that it was an investment and one that I wasn't taking lightly as a single family income household.

I talked to my husband about it and told him that this wasn't something that I wanted, it was something that I needed.

He was like, are you sure?

I wanted to change, I wanted to make a difference — in my core I knew I had the ability to help other people. I was sure.

Things really changed for me when it came to the shadow work unit in Holistic Witchery. The importance of changing the inner narrative and re-writing that narrative, that was a life changing moment for me. Looking back at everything I had been through I was able to see exactly where my trouble was stemming from and put it in my own words and see things differently going forward.

That's when everything just started opening up. I was feeling better physically, I was happy, and I was ready to set my intention.

When I started Holistic Witchery I was prompted to come up with three different intentions. I was struggling to put them together and Sara asked me if I could use one word to tie them all together. That word was balance.

I became time intentional and made a daily schedule and a household schedule that stuck! I even laminated them so I could use dry erase markers to use them again and again.

As the end of Holistic Witchery came, I remember Sara mentioning that the TSE customer support was answering up to 200 emails a day. In that moment I had the confidence to reach out and say I'm here if you need help in any way. I saw what TSE did for me and I wanted to be a part of that for someone else.

Everyone in my life has noticed the transformation.

Now I work at The Sisters Enchanted and love to help people in our customer service inbox. My favorite emails are ones questioning terminology or religion around the word 'witch'.

Being able to explain to them about the empowerment and independence around the word and the history of it makes my day. Seeing those people have their own lightbulb moments is powerful.

In the summer of 2022 Sara looked at me on a Zoom call and told me she was proud of me. It's one thing to hear that from someone like your parents and another to hear it from someone on the outskirts of your life.

Dreaming outside the box only happens when you allow yourself to experience discomfort.

Chapter Five

Crowdsourcing your future

Christine embarked on a journey fueled by a powerful intention—to feel fully supported in her life. Little did she know that this path would be adorned with both triumphs and perceived failures, ultimately leading her to a treasure chest brimming with self-discovery and invaluable insights.

In her relentless pursuit of growth and expansion, Christine began to unravel the essence of her being. Each step she took along this transformative journey unveiled a wealth of knowledge about herself—knowledge that held immeasurable value. Every setback, every perceived failure, became a stepping stone for self-reflection and a catalyst for personal evolution.

Through the dance of intention setting, integration, introspection, and envisioning, Christine nurtured her intuition. Like a flower in spring, her intuitive senses blossomed, guiding her through the labyrinth of life's uncertainties. With every cycle of expansion, her trust in herself grew stronger, fortified by a deep-seated belief in the realm of possibilities that lay before her.

Christine came to understand that she was inherently worthy—worthy of love, abundance, and success. This profound realization illuminated her path, infusing her with an unshakable sense of power.

As she tapped into her innate wholeness, she began to embrace her authentic self, shedding the layers of self-doubt and societal conditioning that had once held her captive.

At the heart of Christine's journey lies intuition—a vibrant force that flows through her, propelling her forward and whispering words of wisdom. Through her commitment to the expansion rhythm, she hones her intuitive abilities, sharpening her inner compass. This rhythmic dance of intention, integration, insight, and ideation empowers her to course-correct swiftly and effortlessly.

As Christine becomes more attuned to her intuition, she experiences a heightened agility—an ability to navigate life's twists and turns with grace and ease. No longer tethered to the weight of external expectations, she embraces a state of balance, where she observes life's circumstances with neutrality. From this place of centeredness, she moves with confidence and clarity, guided by the profound wisdom residing within her.

In trusting her intuition, Christine discovers a boundless wellspring of resilience and adaptability. The expansion rhythm becomes her guiding light, propelling her towards a life infused with purpose and fulfillment. With each iteration of this rhythm, her inner fire burns brighter, igniting a path illuminated by her innate brilliance.

As Christine continues on her journey, she realizes that the true measure of success lies not in the absence of setbacks or failures, but in the depth of her self-awareness and her unwavering commitment to her future self. Each step she takes brings her closer to embodying her authentic essence, unleashing her true potential, and creating a life of profound joy and abundance.

In Christine's relentless pursuit of feeling fully supported, she discovers the transformative power of intuition. Her journey serves as a testament to the resilience of the human spirit and the infinite capacity for self-discovery. As she embraces the expansion rhythm, she becomes a beacon of inspiration—an example of the extraordinary possibilities that lie within each of us, waiting to be unlocked.

* * *

Remember in Chapter One when we discussed executive function skills? We are all born intuitive, with an inner compass that points to our truth. If that truth doesn't match up with an external standard, we are led to believe that our way of being and inner knowing is wrong, Our bodies don't sit still enough, our minds don't work the right way, and we don't say the right things. We are taken farther and farther from self trust and intuition as we grow.

As if that's not enough to contend with, we live in a world where instant gratification and quick answers are sought after, it is all too common for individuals to turn to external sources for guidance and solutions. People often find themselves crowdsourcing advice from friends, seeking counsel from psychics or therapists, and desperately longing for someone—anyone—to provide them with the answers they seek.

The consequences of this reliance on external validation and guidance are far-reaching. Sleepless nights are spent agonizing over missed signs and analyzing every interaction, searching for hidden meanings in every word, gesture, and glance. Precious time slips away as individuals tirelessly read between the lines, hoping to find the answers they crave.

Yet, there is a different path—one that Christine, and you, are embarking upon. It is the path of profound transformation and self-empowerment, rooted in the cultivation of an expansion rhythm that strengthens intuition and unlocks the answers that lie within.

By engaging in the beautifully life-changing work of creating an expansion rhythm, Christine, and you, are actively shaping your own destinies. You recognize that the answers you seek are not found outside yourself, but are already present within your own being, waiting to be heard and acknowledged.

Developing this expansion rhythm becomes a powerful catalyst for personal growth and self-discovery. It is through this intentional practice of expanding awareness, aligning with inner truth, and embracing growth that the clarity and insight needed to navigate life's challenges are revealed.

Gone are the days of relying solely on external sources for guidance. You, and our character Christine, understand that the next right step, the path to an aligned and purposeful life, and the inherent ability to create that life reside within the expansion rhythm that is being cultivated.

The journey towards knowing oneself deeply and finding the answers within is a deep undertaking. It requires dedication, patience, and a willingness to trust in one's own intuitive guidance. Through the expansion rhythm outlined in this book, Christine, and you, embark on a transformative journey that empowers you to reclaim your own agency and create a life of meaning and fulfillment.

No longer beholden to the opinions or expectations of others, you step into your own power, guided by your inner compass. You understand that the true path to knowing what is right for you lies in the expansion of your own consciousness, not in seeking validation or answers from an external audience.

By embracing this expansion rhythm, you are on a remarkable journey of self-discovery, where you uncover your true purpose and the limitless potential that resides within. You are no longer adrift in a sea of uncertainty but instead find solace and direction in the depths of your own being. You realize that the stories that made you who you are were written by other people. People who had not done their inner work and people striving to meet impossible societal expectations.

As you continue to deepen your expansion rhythm and strengthen your intuition, every reader of this book becomes a beacon of inspiration for others. Your stories serve as reminders that the path to self-discovery and a life of alignment begins within, and that the answers we seek are waiting to be unearthed through the intentional cultivation of our own expansion rhythm.

Journal Prompts:

What does it feel like to know, to trust, to believe? To remember you are magic, powerful, and worthy just as you are?

Reflect on a time when you sought external validation or guidance. How did it affect your decision-making process? How did it make you feel?

Write about a situation where you trusted your intuition or inner guidance. What was the outcome? How did it differ from times when you relied on external advice?

What does the concept of an "expansion rhythm" mean to you? How can you cultivate this rhythm in your daily life to strengthen your intuition and self-awareness?

Describe your journey of self-discovery so far. What have you learned about yourself? How has this journey influenced your understanding of your purpose and potential?

5i Expansion:

The fifth and final i in our transformative journey is Intuition. This refers to your inner wisdom, your internal voice, and your personal compass that is constantly communicating with you. It's a whisper from your soul, a nudge from your subconscious, guiding you towards your true path. However, hearing this voice, trusting its wisdom, and taking action based on its guidance is a journey in itself. It's a journey that requires patience, openness, and a deep sense of trust in oneself.

As you move through the 5i Expansion model, you'll find yourself returning to this journey of intuition again and again. Each cycle through the model strengthens your intuitive abilities, amplifying the voice of your inner wisdom. Over time, this voice becomes louder and clearer, making it easier for you to hear and trust it. This iterative process is not a one-time event but a continuous cycle of growth and expansion that deepens your connection with your intuition.

There's a common misconception that intuition is a special gift that only some people possess, or that you can do certain things to become more intuitive. However, the reality is quite different. Intuition is not exclusive to a select few, nor is it something that can be acquired through specific actions or practices. Rather, intuition is a natural part of the human experience. It's inherent in all of us.

The key difference lies in trust. Some people trust their intuition and themselves, while others don't. This trust, or lack thereof, can significantly impact one's ability to tap into their intuition and use it as a guide. Trusting oneself is the bedrock upon which an aligned life is built. It's the foundation that supports the journey towards self-awareness and personal growth.

As you become more self-aware and flow through the 5i Expansion model, your intuition naturally grows. It's like a muscle that strengthens with use. The more you listen to it, trust it, and act on its guidance, the stronger it becomes. This growth in intuition is not a result of doing something specific to be more intuitive, but rather a natural byproduct of the journey towards self-awareness and alignment.

In essence, intuition is your internal GPS, guiding you towards your true north. It's a powerful tool that, when trusted and acted upon, can lead you towards a life of alignment, fulfillment, and authenticity. So, as you continue your journey through the 5i Expansion model, remember to listen to your intuition, trust its wisdom, and let it guide you towards your true path.

Embodiment:

Rest. Rest your mind, rest your body, and rest your soul. Allow yourself to reset, because you've only just begun.

Make Magic:

Materials Needed:

- A small bowl of water (representing Water)
- A feather or incense (representing Air)
- A candle (representing Fire)
- A small stone or crystal (representing Earth)
- A quiet, comfortable space for the spell

Instructions:

1. Preparation: Find a quiet, comfortable space where you won't be disturbed. Arrange your materials in front of you.
2. Invocation of the Elements: Begin by invoking the four elements. Hold the bowl of water and say, "I call upon the element of Water, to cleanse and heal my emotions." Hold the feather or incense and say, "I call upon the element of Air, to clear my mind and bring clarity." Light the candle and say, "I call upon the element of Fire, to ignite my inner strength and courage." Hold the stone or crystal and say, "I call upon the element of Earth, to ground me and provide stability."
3. Affirmation: Close your eyes and take a few deep breaths. Visualize a light within you, representing your inner self. Say the following affirmation, "I trust my inner self. I trust my intuition. I know the way forward."
4. Visualization: Visualize the light within you growing brighter with each breath. Imagine it guiding you forward on your path, illuminating any obstacles and showing you the way.
5. Closing: When you feel ready, say, "I thank the elements for their guidance. I move forward with trust and confidence."

Extinguish the candle, put away the feather or incense, return the water and stone to nature if possible.

6. Reflection: Spend a few moments reflecting on the spell. How do you feel? Do you feel a stronger sense of trust in your inner self?

Real Life Story:

Sharon B.

I would rather be me than have to be something else for someone else.

I joined The Sisters Enchanted in the summer of 2020, right in the midst of the pandemic. I had become so isolated being home with the kids before the pandemic and now it was even worse.

If my husband was even thirty minutes late getting home from work I would be pissed.

As a stay-at-home mom I had completely lost my identity. Before kids I was a school counselor and felt like I was helping people and doing something good in the world. I went from providing suicide assessments and participating in active shooter drills with a caseload of 350 students to being home with the same two kids day in and day out.

Who am I now?

Who am I and what is my life if I'm not a school counselor?

These are the questions I was tackling when I stumbled upon The Sisters Enchanted.

Searching for myself and with time on my hands due to the pandemic, I pulled out my tarot cards that I had had since high school. People in my life caught wind of this and started requesting readings.

At that point I knew that I wanted to dive more into tarot. In high school I had been a witchy-woo kid who would rather be reading mythology than young adult fiction and I felt this bubbling again.

I saw an ad for the Tarot Throwdown class taught by TSE and knew that this was it. I knew how to use the cards but had never really focused on any kind of training.

Through this experience I found myself again. I loved Tarot Throwdown and the idea of reading intuitively while gaining background knowledge and basic understanding of the cards was huge.

I had worked from guidebooks but never trusted myself enough to go without the guidebook. It was less, "here's step by step how," and more, "here's the info, figure out a way that works for you". I'm a rule follower so the permission to try different strategies and figure out what worked for me was huge.

This led me to realize that I could fully create my own identity based on what worked for me and what didn't.

I went on to join Holistic Witchery that October and, naturally, loved the divination unit. The everyday magic part was fantastic and gave me loads of ideas for things to do everyday (and reinforced to me that I don't like being in the kitchen!). The program reframed all the witchy-woo from high school and made it fit into my life as a mom of two kids and a wife.

Before taking Tarot Throwdown I had been thinking about starting my own business so when Sara offered a program on getting an online business started, I was all in! This is when my husband and friends really started to notice a huge change in me. I was more animated again, excited to get up in the morning, and had something that was MINE. I now had something to share with my friends (who don't have kids) and could contribute to the conversation.

I had become muted and that changed. What I learned in this program helped me increase my revenue from 2021 to 2022 by 83.6%!

My biggest aha during my time with The Sisters Enchanted has been to learn how to do things in a way that aligns with who I truly am. I learned to consider if what I was about to embark on really fit with me and my life. The Sisters Enchanted is all about personal choice. They give you all of this amazing information and then invite you to be brave enough to do something with it.

Now I am more confident. Feel like I have reclaimed my identity, and know much more about who I am. Before The Sisters Enchanted I was willing to sacrifice a lot of who I was in order to please other people and even though I have lost relationships along the way in this journey, I feel like it was a good thing because they weren't worth having in the first place.

The Sisters Enchanted gave me the courage and the confidence to make those choices and stand up for myself and be the independent person that I am today, living in my own truth. I have a thriving business now as well, thank you very much.

You already know the answers. Learn to trust. Learn to listen. Learn to believe.

Conclusion

Two left feet

You were Born Magic.

We all were.

Some may be shrinking their energy and not seeing this innate quality. Some are negotiating their energy and beginning to remember that there is a "them" below the surface. Others have done a bit of this and a bit of that on their growth journey, are maintaining their energy, and know they are worthy of a delightful life.

The people who are expanding... those are the ones who have embraced their authenticity, made peace with the stories that created them, and are living a life that feels utterly enchanted (not perfect, but enchanted all the same). They know they were Born Magic.

How do you know what energy you're standing in?

If this book felt like one giant wake up call then it's a good chance you're in the shrinking or negotiating stage of energetic alignment.

If you find yourself nodding your head and thinking, "louder for the people in the back!" on repeat in your head, then you may be at the maintaining or expanding stage of energetic alignment.

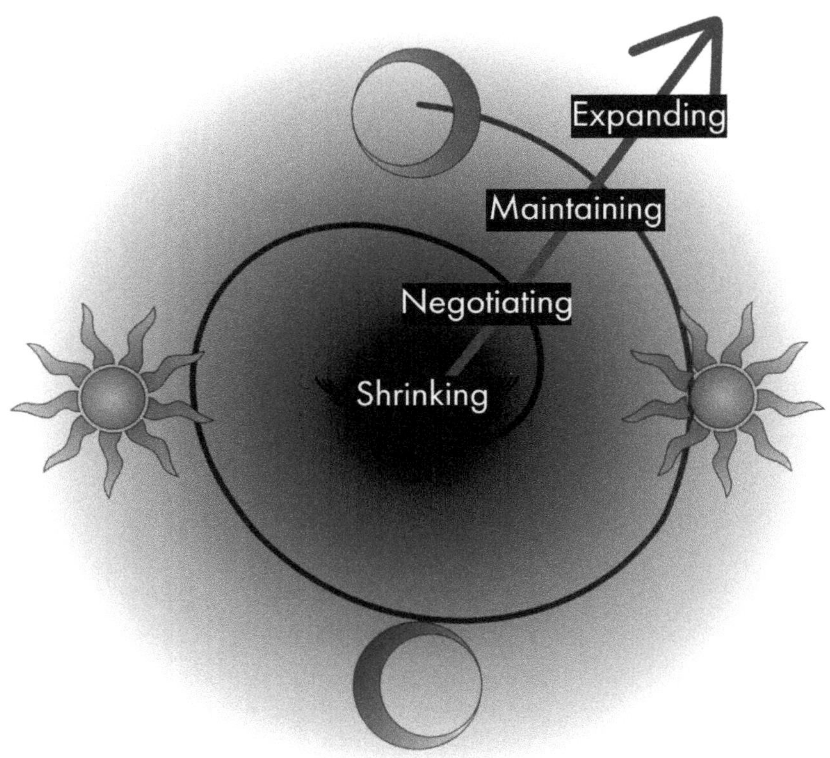

If you're a person who feels like you are shrinking or negotiating your energy right now and want to crawl in bed and turn the lights off, hold up. This is a beautiful place to be. It's like looking at a blank canvas.

The dance with who you were, who you are, and who you will be is just beginning, and it's going to be a little less salsa and a lot more two left feet in the beginning.

Just reading this book and shifting the way you think is a first step toward claiming your birthright as a person who is worthy of living a life of alignment that feels like joy, abundance, and relaxation. One that feels ALIVE.

If you are maintaining or expanding your energy, get into community with others doing the same. There's a saying that you are the sum of the five people you spend the most time with. I believe you are the sum of their energy. Be in energy with other people who are living an aligned life and acting as if they were born for relaxation, joy, and abundance.

Here's the thing — over time we will all fall into and out of each level of expansion again and again and again. Whether it's getting a new job, retiring, becoming an empty nester, leaving or starting a relationship... Whatever the thing is, you will inevitably come face to face with a situation that unearths an old story and sends you back to the beginning, if even for a short time.

This is why developing a rhythm of expansion in your life is non-negotiable in your quest for alignment. You are not a building made of steel that doesn't ever shift or move. You are more like a sandcastle (and I mean that in a very good way). You can be molded into anything you desire but can also be taken down by a rogue wave. And, you can be built back up again.

Rhythm, community, and awareness will always lead to more alignment and a life that feels like magic. I know this because it's how I, a girl from a broken home with a broken soul to match, have grown into a person who lives a life that others can't begin to imagine.

I know this because I've worked with thousands of people who have changed just one thing in their lives that has brought on a sense of harmony they haven't experienced in ages. I know this because I've worked with hundreds of kids and have seen, firsthand, how the stories they are being told about what they are and are not good at is creating their sense of self.

You know you were Born Magic. Now you must Stay Magic.

Believe in the inherent magic you possess and embrace the responsibility of nurturing your inner light. The notion of staying magic transcends the mundane obligations of life, urging us to remain connected to the spark that ignites our souls.

Like a radiant flame, our inner light has the power to illuminate not only our own lives but also the lives of others. Yet, the key lies in first nurturing our own flame, for only then can we share its transformative energy with the world. It is in the act of staying magic that we embody our unique essence and allow it to guide our journey.

Staying magic is not without its challenges. Life presents us with hardships and moments when our inner flame may waver. Yet, these moments serve as opportunities for growth and resilience. By acknowledging and honoring the shadows, we can reignite our flame with renewed strength and radiance.

Reading this book is the first step.

Living this book is the second.

Onward.

The dance with who you were, who you are, and who you will be is just beginning, and it's going to be a little less salsa and a lot more two left feet in the beginning.

Now what?

Discover whether you are shrinking or expanding your sacred energy by taking the Life Alignment Quiz.

The first set of questions relate to your Soul's Purpose and Intention Setting:

- Do you feel like you have a sense of clarity about what you want in life five years from now? YES / NO
- Do you set intentions for how you want to feel and re-visit that intention regularly? YES / NO
- Do you feel like there is an identifiable rhythm to your energy and life? YES / NO
- Do you find it easy to plan your day even when life feels really overwhelming? YES / NO
- Do you often feel like the next step for you is just around the corner and like it's easy to see what to do next? YES / NO

Total YES ____

The second set of questions relate to Self-Awareness and how you take action on your intentions:

- Do you feel like you know how to manage your time so you can lead your family and/or do well at work and still have plenty of time for yourself? YES / NO

- Do you know how to set goals and actually achieve them? YES / NO
- Do you think you have more strengths than weaknesses? YES / NO
- Are you able to keep your sense of inner peace and balance no matter how those around you are feeling? YES / NO
- Do you set and enforce boundaries in your life? YES / NO

Total YES ____

The third set of questions relate to Emotional Wounds and the ability to use this insight for expansion:

- Do you feel like you are safely able to be your most authentic self? YES / NO
- Do you feel like you embody deep confidence in yourself? YES / NO
- Do you feel like you trust yourself to know the way forward? YES / NO
- Can you clearly see where your desires and actions are not in alignment? YES / NO
- Do you feel like you are able to become the person you want to become without your past holding you back? YES / NO

Total YES ____

The fourth set of questions relate to Future Self ideation:

- Do you feel like you can clearly see how your life experiences have made you who you are? YES / NO

- Do you feel like you are surrounded and supported by the kind of people who are fully aligned with your soul's purpose? YES / NO
- Do you feel like you know how to become the person you want to become? YES / NO
- Do you feel like you are leaving a positive impact on the world? YES / NO
- Are you able to work toward becoming who you want to become without the fear of letting other people down holding you back? YES / NO

Total YES ____

The fifth and final set of questions is about Inner Knowing and intuition:

- Do you trust your gut when it speaks to you? YES / NO
- Do you make decisions without seeking validation from others? YES / NO
- Do you believe you are your own best friend? YES / NO
- Do you trust you are learning exactly what you need to learn right now? YES / NO
- Do you believe you have valuable inner wisdom? YES / NO

Total YES ____

Results: Add up the number of yes answers for each of the five sections individually. You will have a 0-5 score for each of the five sections.

- 0-2 you are Shrinking your Energy in that area
- 3 you are Negotiating your Energy in that area
- 4 you are Maintaining your Energy in that area
- 5 you are Expanding your Energy in that area

Now you've taken the quiz, scan the QR code to get a free curated podcast playlist to help you grow into the next level of expansion.

5i Templates

This method works, and I'm here to help

Sometimes when you're really stuck it's helpful to have a starting point. That's what these templates are. They are helpful resources to get you moving when you're not sure what step to take and just can't get out of your own head.

I teach the 5i framework in depth in my Holistic Witchery program. This is where I combine secular spirituality with modern mysticism and practical tools to help you create a life that feels utterly enchanted even when everything is chaotic, uncertain, and hard.

Consider joining the program with the 1,000+ other women who have come before you to deepen into this work.

For now, you'll find ten templates in this book that you can turn to when you just don't know which way is up.

1. 5i Your Family Communication
2. 5i Your Career Transition
3. 5i Your Financial Investment
4. 5i Your Relationship Transition
5. 5i Your Groove
6. 5i Your Healthy Lifestyle

7. 5i Your Assertiveness
8. 5i Your Relationship Boundaries
9. 5i Your Imposter Syndrome
10. 5i Your Libido Boost

5i Your Family Communication

I intend to feel... (choose one):

- I intend to feel heard.
- I intend to feel understood.
- I intend to feel patient.
- I intend to feel compassionate.

Integrate (choose one):

- Practice active listening during family conversations.
- Create a list of conversation topics that you feel comfortable discussing with your family.
- Set boundaries for conversations, such as no interruptions or respecting each other's viewpoints.
- Plan a family activity that encourages open and honest communication.

Insight (choose one):

- Where did I meet resistance in improving communication?
- What old communication patterns do I need to release?
- What uncomfortable feelings arose during family conversations?
- What am I really proud of in my efforts to communicate better?

Ideate (choose one):

- Change the decor in a room where communication often goes sideways to create a peaceful environment.
- Create a tangible anchor (like a symbol or a phrase) that reminds you of your communication goals.
- Practice gratitude for the positive communication moments you've had with your family.

- Write a letter to a family member expressing your feelings (you don't have to send it).

Intuition (choose one):

- Choose three tarot cards to represent your current communication style, your desired style, and the path between them. Write about this journey.
- Meditate on the feeling of successful communication. How does it feel in your body? What thoughts come up?
- Pay homage to an entity that embodies effective communication for you. This could be a deity, a natural element, or even a fictional character.
- Write a letter to yourself from the perspective of your future self who communicates effectively with the family. What advice do they have for you?

5i Your Career Transition

I intend to feel... (choose one):

- I intend to feel excited.
- I intend to feel confident.
- I intend to feel prepared.
- I intend to feel fulfilled.

Integrate (choose one):

- Create an exit plan from your current situation.
- Outline your ideal weekly rhythm and schedule to make space for the next move.
- Create a list of your strengths.
- Identify the skills and experiences you have that will transfer to your new career.

Insight (choose one):

- Where did I meet resistance in considering a career change?
- What fears or doubts about the career change do I need to release?
- What uncomfortable feelings arose during this process?
- Where am I discounting my skills, strengths, and abilities?

Ideate (choose one):

- Write a list of affirmations to help you close the door on one chapter and open a door to the next.
- Create a tangible anchor (like a symbol or a phrase) that represents your career goals.
- Practice gratitude for the experiences and skills your current career has given you.
- Plan steps for the next week that will move you closer to your career change.

Intuition (choose one):

- Choose three tarot cards to represent your current career, your desired career, and the path between them. Write about this journey.
- Meditate on the feeling of working in your desired career. How does it feel in your body? What thoughts come up?
- Pay homage to an entity that embodies the spirit of your desired career. This could be a deity, a natural element, or even a fictional character.
- Write a letter to yourself from the perspective of your future self who has successfully transitioned careers. What advice do they have for you?

5i Your Financial Investment

I intend to feel... (choose one):

- I intend to feel confident.
- I intend to feel secure.
- I intend to feel informed.
- I intend to feel prepared.

Integrate (choose one):

- Set up automated payments or recurring money allocation to make it happen.
- Speak with a financial advisor or someone who has made a similar investment.
- Create a detailed financial plan that includes this investment.
- Identify your financial goals and how this investment aligns with them.

Insight (choose one):

- Where did I meet resistance in considering this investment?
- What fears or doubts about the investment do I need to release?
- What uncomfortable feelings arose during this process?
- What stories about my worth or capability have surfaced during this process?

Ideate (choose one):

- Write a list of ways to increase income that you haven't yet tried.
- Create a tangible anchor (like a symbol or a phrase) that represents your financial goals.
- Practice gratitude for the financial resources you have that allow you to consider this investment.

- Write a confidence ritual or prayer to remind yourself of your strengths, worth, and abilities.

Intuition (choose one):

- Choose three tarot cards to represent your current financial state, your desired state after the investment, and the path between them. Write about this journey.
- Meditate on the feeling of making a successful investment. How does it feel in your body? What thoughts come up?
- Pay homage to an entity that embodies wealth and prosperity for you. This could be a deity, a natural element, or even a fictional character.
- Write a letter to yourself from the perspective of your future self who has successfully made the investment. What advice do they have for you?

5i Your Relationship Transition

I intend to feel... (choose one):

- I intend to feel liberated.
- I intend to feel healed.
- I intend to feel hopeful.
- I intend to feel self-loving.

Integrate (choose one):

- Plan activities for the next week that celebrate your independence and individuality.
- Create a list of lessons learned from the relationship.
- Practice self-care activities that make you feel loved and cherished.
- Write a list of action steps to take to create space between yourself and the version of the relationship that is ending.

Insight (choose one):

- Where did I meet resistance in moving on from the relationship?
- What emotions or attachments do I need to release?
- What uncomfortable feelings arose during this process?
- Where am I tying my worth to the failure or success of this relationship? What do I subconsciously believe it is saying about me?

Ideate (choose one):

- Create a tangible anchor (like a symbol or a phrase) that represents your journey of moving on.
- Practice gratitude for the growth and experiences the relationship brought you.
- Write a letter to your past self in the relationship (you don't have to send it).
- Identify your needs and wants for future relationships.

Intuition (choose one):

- Choose three tarot cards to represent your past relationship, your current singlehood, and your future love life. Write about this journey.
- Meditate on the feeling of being out of that relationship or in a different version of it and content. How does it feel in your body? What thoughts come up?
- Pay homage to an entity that embodies self-love and independence for you. This could be a deity, a natural element, or even a fictional character.
- Write a letter to yourself from the perspective of your future self who has successfully moved on. What advice do they have for you?

5i Your Groove

I intend to feel... (choose one):

- I intend to feel energized.
- I intend to feel passionate.
- I intend to feel confident.
- I intend to feel joyful.

Integrate (choose one):

- Engage in an activity that you used to love but haven't done in a while.
- Create a playlist of songs that make you feel alive and vibrant.
- Practice daily affirmations that boost your self-esteem and confidence.
- Identify what activities, people, or situations drain your energy and consider ways to minimize them.

Insight (choose one):

- Where did I meet resistance in trying to regain my groove?
- What negative beliefs or habits do I need to release to get my groove back?
- What uncomfortable feelings arose during this process?
- What subconscious stories or beliefs surfaced that made me feel like I didn't deserve to be in my groove?

Ideate (choose one):

- What is a creative way to inject more fun and energy into my life in the next cycle?
- Create a tangible anchor (like a symbol or a phrase) that represents your vibrant, groovy self.
- Practice gratitude for the moments when you've felt your groove.

- Create a mandala or grid that feels energetically expansive to you and allow it to charge up your energy and get you excited again.

Intuition (choose one):

- Choose three tarot cards to represent your current state, your desired groovy state, and the path between them. Write about this journey.
- Meditate on the feeling of being in your groove. How does it feel in your body? What thoughts come up?
- Pay homage to an entity that embodies vibrancy and energy for you. This could be a deity, a natural element, or even a fictional character.
- Write a letter to yourself from the perspective of your future self who has successfully gotten their groove back. What advice do they have for you?

5i Your Healthy Lifestyle

I intend to feel... (choose one):

- I intend to feel energized.
- I intend to feel strong.
- I intend to feel balanced.
- I intend to feel nourished.

Integrate (choose one):

- Incorporate a new healthy habit into your daily routine, such as drinking more water or taking a walk.
- Create a meal plan that includes whole foods you enjoy.
- Practice mindfulness or meditation to promote mental health.
- Identify unhealthy habits you'd like to change and brainstorm healthier alternatives.

Insight (choose one):

- Where did I meet resistance in making healthy changes?
- What unhealthy patterns or beliefs do I need to release?
- What uncomfortable feelings arose during this process?
- Where am I holding the belief that I'm not good enough for a change or that it's too hard and I'll never follow through?

Ideate (choose one):

- Dream about a day where you feel great in your mind and body. Create a vision board to represent that day.
- Create a tangible anchor (like a symbol or a phrase) that represents your commitment to health.
- Practice gratitude for your body and all the amazing things it does for you.
- List activities that promote physical, mental, and emotional health. Decorate an intention jar and put the activities in it on separate slips of paper. As you remove and complete

each one, add a stone into the jar. Keep doing this until the jar is full and release the stones back to the Earth in a ceremony for yourself.

Intuition (choose one):

- Choose three tarot cards to represent your current health, your desired state of health, and the path between them. Write about this journey.
- Meditate on the feeling of being in a healthy, vibrant body. How does it feel in your body? What thoughts come up?
- Pay homage to an entity that embodies health and vitality for you. This could be a deity, a natural element, or even a fictional character.
- Write a letter to yourself from the perspective of your future self who has successfully adopted a healthy lifestyle. What advice do they have for you?

5i Your Assertiveness

I intend to feel... (choose one):

- I intend to feel confident.
- I intend to feel respected.
- I intend to feel heard.
- I intend to feel empowered.

Integrate (choose one):

- Practice assertive communication techniques, such as using "I" statements.
- Create a list of your rights and boundaries in interpersonal relationships.
- Role-play assertive responses to situations where you typically struggle.
- Record yourself asking for something that you want and listen back to it. Do this again and again until you feel confident and comfortable.

Insight (choose one):

- Where did I meet resistance in being assertive?
- What fears or beliefs about assertiveness do I need to release?
- What uncomfortable feelings arose during this process?
- Where am I holding on to a martyr or 'good girl' complex that is keeping me from being assertive?

Ideate (choose one):

- Identify situations where you feel you could have been more assertive and consider how you might handle them differently in the future.
- Create a tangible anchor (like a symbol or a phrase) that represents your assertive self.

- Practice gratitude for the moments when you've successfully been assertive.
- Connect to the energy of a tree or large boulder. Notice how they take up all the space they desire without saying a word (since they can't speak, obviously). How can you create that same sense of empowerment within yourself? Consider printing an image of a tree or finding a rock that speaks to you and keeping it with you as you work on being assertive.

Intuition (choose one):

- Choose three tarot cards to represent your current assertiveness, your desired level of assertiveness, and the path between them. Write about this journey.
- Meditate on the feeling of being assertive. How does it feel in your body? What thoughts come up?
- Pay homage to an entity that embodies assertiveness for you. This could be a deity, a natural element, or even a fictional character.
- Write a letter to yourself from the perspective of your future self who has successfully become more assertive. What advice do they have for you?

5i Your Relationship Boundaries

I intend to feel... (choose one):

- I intend to feel respected.
- I intend to feel understood.
- I intend to feel secure.
- I intend to feel balanced.

Integrate (choose one):

- Have a conversation with your partner about your needs and boundaries.
- Practice feeling an energetic bubble around you that acts as a boundary keeping out negative, undesired, and unhelpful energy.
- Practice assertive communication techniques when discussing boundaries.
- Identify situations where your boundaries were crossed and consider how you might handle them differently in the future.

Insight (choose one):

- Where did I meet resistance in setting boundaries?
- What fears or beliefs about setting boundaries do I need to release?
- What uncomfortable feelings arose during this process?
- Where am I justifying not setting boundaries or repeating past cycles of not setting boundaries?

Ideate (choose one):

- Write a letter to your partner outlining your boundaries (you don't have to send it).
- Create a tangible anchor (like a symbol or a phrase) that represents your commitment to your boundaries.

- Practice gratitude for the moments when your boundaries have been respected.
- Cast an energetic circle or write the thing you are protecting on a piece of paper and create a circle around it with natural items like stones or seeds. Allow this to be your energetic guide post for maintaining your boundaries.

Intuition (choose one):

- Choose three tarot cards to represent your current relationship boundaries, your desired boundaries, and the path between them. Write about this journey.
- Meditate on the feeling of having your boundaries respected. How does it feel in your body? What thoughts come up?
- Pay homage to an entity that embodies respect and boundaries for you. This could be a deity, a natural element, or even a fictional character.
- Write a letter to yourself from the perspective of your future self who has successfully set boundaries. What advice do they have for you?

5i Your Imposter Syndrome

I intend to feel... (choose one):

- I intend to feel confident.
- I intend to feel capable.
- I intend to feel authentic.
- I intend to feel valued.

Integrate (choose one):

- Write a list of your achievements and skills to remind yourself of your capabilities.
- Practice positive affirmations that boost your self-esteem and counter negative self-talk.
- Seek feedback from trusted colleagues or mentors to gain an objective perspective on your abilities.
- Look around you and make a list of what is true. You are uniquely you doing the thing you are doing at the moment. Ground yourself in tangible reality.

Insight (choose one):

- Where did I meet resistance in overcoming imposter syndrome?
- What fears or beliefs about my abilities do I need to release?
- What uncomfortable feelings arose during this process?
- What inner child stories are coming up that are making me feel like I'm not living as my authentic self?

Ideate (choose one):

- Identify situations where you felt like an imposter and consider how you might reframe these experiences positively. Create oracle cards from these stories that you can refer to as needed.
- Create a tangible anchor (like a symbol or a phrase) that represents your authentic, capable self.

- Practice gratitude for the skills and experiences that make you uniquely qualified.
- Roll a beeswax candle while feeling into the energy of competency and skill. Burn the candle to release the feelings of inadequacy.

Intuition (choose one):

- Choose three tarot cards to represent your current state of imposter syndrome, your desired state of confidence, and the path between them. Write about this journey.
- Meditate on the feeling of being confident and authentic. How does it feel in your body? What thoughts come up?
- Pay homage to an entity that embodies confidence and authenticity for you. This could be a deity, a natural element, or even a fictional character.
- Write a letter to yourself from the perspective of your future self who has successfully overcome imposter syndrome. What advice do they have for you?

5i Your Libido

I intend to feel... (choose one):

- I intend to feel passionate.
- I intend to feel sensual.
- I intend to feel energized.
- I intend to feel connected.

Integrate (choose one):

- Incorporate regular physical activity into your routine, as exercise can boost libido.
- Practice mindfulness or meditation to reduce stress, which can impact libido.
- Create a romantic or sensual atmosphere to stimulate desire.
- Schedule in a time for this connection to occur so it isn't forgotten or bypassed.

Insight (choose one):

- Where did I meet resistance in trying to increase my libido?
- What fears or beliefs about my sexuality do I need to release?
- What uncomfortable feelings arose during this process?
- Where am I not feeling supported, respected, or heard by the other person in this relationship and how is that impacting my ability to relax and have fun?

Ideate (choose one):

- What is a creative way to stimulate my senses?
- Create a tangible anchor (like a symbol or a phrase) that represents your sensual self.
- Practice gratitude for the body you have and for all that it is capable of and all that it has experienced.

- Create an environment that feels sacred and sensual. This can include a room and the clothing or jewelry you put on your body. Daydream about what it feels like to feel like a passionate, desirable, and sensual person in this environment.

Intuition (choose one):

- Choose three tarot cards to represent your current libido, your desired libido, and the path between them. Write about this journey.
- Meditate on the feeling of being in tune with your sexual energy. How does it feel in your body? What thoughts come up?
- Pay homage to an entity that embodies passion and sensuality for you. This could be a deity, a natural element, or even a fictional character.
- Write a letter to yourself from the perspective of your future self who has successfully increased their libido. What advice do they have for you?

Resources

Don't go it alone

Life Alignment Quiz

Identify where you are shrinking or expanding your sacred energy using our online Life Alignment Quiz.

After you take the quiz you'll get your result and a curated podcast suggestion to get you started on the path to greater life alignment.

Expansion Archetypes

Are you a Mapper, Wanderer, Adventurer, Dreamer, or Seer?

Your Expansion Archetype speaks to how you manifest AND how you sabotage.

Uncover your archetype and explore shadows, potential, and even relationships like never before.

Holistic Witchery

Sacred Seeing, Modern Mysticism, and Cognitive & Positive Psychology come together in our life-giving Holistic Witchery program. Using our 5i Expansion Spiral we teach participants how to set intentions, trust themselves, and uncover who they are underneath everything they were told they should be. With over 1,000 students this course is the foundation you've been looking for.

Community and Coaching

In our Enchanted Journey membership and Enchanted Journey mastermind we support a vast community of Magic Makers on their expansion, spirituality, and connection to self. In the membership participants are supported through live classes, a vault of learning pathways, and community space holding. The upgraded mastermind option includes 1:1 guidance and mentorship along with deep thought work and small group connection.

Magical Self-Care Book

Cast boundaries, create a strong foundation, and conjure a life that supports you in every way. This book was on the Amazon bestseller list with big names like Tony Robbins and Brené Brown on release date and is a quick read that will have a long-lasting impact on your life. Released in 2022, it can be found online wherever books are sold.

Journal by the Moon Book

Begin journaling, work with the moon, and come home to yourself. This book is one part journal and one part "how to journal". With the book comes digital access to moon practices for every moon phase through every zodiac sign. Find it online wherever books are sold.

Scan the QR code below for more information and for bonus resources created just for this book.

SCAN ME

About the Author

Waves emphatically from the back of the book

The dirty kitchen floor momentarily distracted me from my own crying. A puddle of tears had formed and for an instant I stopped the torrential flow of salt water pouring from my eyes long enough to wonder when it had last been cleaned.

In 2014 I had been thrust into the wild world of self-employment. At seven months pregnant I was sort-of laid off. The small business I had been working for was closing my office and the next closest was over an hour away. I had three choices:

- Commute that distance driving straight toward New York City every day (this was an immediate hard pass).
- Begin applying to work as a public school teacher (I was a certified teacher and had been working in education and this option seemed less than thrilling).
- Go on my own and open my own business doing what I had been doing for the past few years (we have a winner!).

You don't know how much grit and tenacity you have until you have no money in the bank, no health insurance, a baby very close to arrival, and a business to start.

Two and a half months later I delivered a baby girl in what was a harrowing experience. After a series of twists and turns I was on an operating table with a ruptured uterus, a non-responsive newborn, and a doctor repeating things like, "I can't leave her this way," and, "it's not working."

Luckily, I would be okay and so would my daughter. It was a miracle.

Six weeks later I had overcome an abscess that put me back in the hospital, two weeks of a drainage tube hanging out of my belly and running into a bag strapped to my leg, a pediatrician swap, and was right back at work.

In 2016 I was ready to begin thinking about baby number two and was tired. I was burnt out from a few not ideal clients and knew that the way to change the lives of kids was actually by changing the lives of the women who impacted them most. The Sisters Enchanted was born in May 2016.

I became pregnant with my son in the fall of 2016 and ran both of my businesses while spending the daytime hours home with my daughter. I was battling low blood sugar, was still without health insurance, and was again so very tired.

In May 2017 my absolutely perfect baby boy was born. I closed my first business and went all in on The Sisters Enchanted.

A few weeks later I was on my kitchen floor with my laptop next to me, a baby crying in my lap, and a toddler pulling my hair. I cried until I couldn't breathe. Then I noticed the dirty floor, took a breath, and started crying again.

This is when I knew something had to change. I had evidence that I was strong and capable (after all, I had already moved mountains under impossible circumstances) but just couldn't seem to get everything moving in the right direction all at once.

From that moment on the floor to the present there were more tears. I became absolutely ruthless in my pursuit of a life that felt joyful, abundant, and relaxed. And I knew that the way to that was through intention, intuition, and everyday magic.

I was right. Now, in 2023 as I write this book, I am infinitely faster at course correcting when I've begun to live out of alignment with myself. And I've been able to help others do the same with my proven 5i Expansion framework.

That's my story and it's why I wrote this book.

I know I'm not the only one who looks around one day and just doesn't understand how life came to be the way it is. I know I'm not the only one who logically knows I'm a smart person and doesn't understand how such a smart, capable person could let it come to this. I know I'm not the only one who has cried a puddle of tears and then realized it was time to mop the floor, hiding the evidence of a moment of weakness, pushing it back down to be dealt with another day.

I wasn't the only one, and you aren't either. I hope this book is the jumpstart that every reader needs to help them realize they were Born Magic and the life they desire is always just around the corner of intention, intuition, and everyday magic.

Now, for the super professional third person version of who I am:

Sara Walka, M.Ed., is a Life Alignment Coach, Executive Function Skills Expert, Psychic Intuitive, and Positive Discipline Educator.

Combining her experience as a Certified Teacher, former sales and marketing rep for a leading food company, and lifelong intuitive and intentional creatrix, she created an approach to help people live with more intention, intuition, and everyday magic that works.

As the Founder and CEO of The Sisters Enchanted, Sara brings this methodology to life in all offerings at The Sisters Enchanted to help women live aligned lives that are joyful, abundant, and relaxed even when chaos reigns, life is uncertain, and everything feels hard.

When not operating The Sisters Enchanted Sara can be found homeschooling her two spicy kids and traveling with those same kids and her husband in their embarrassingly large RV looking for new adventures and great food.

I wasn't the only one, and you aren't either.

Book Bonuses

Scan the QR code on this page and gain access to extra Book Bonuses:

- Born Magic Meditation Series
- Born Magic Printable Journal
- Printable Born Magic Manifesto
- Guide to Creating Your Own Born Magic Manifesto
- Born Magic Music Playlist
- Born Magic Affirmations

Printed in the USA
CPSIA information can be obtained
at www.ICGtesting.com
LVHW071245050923
757075LV00017B/1207

9 798985 814842